THE
CHOICE
IS YOURS

LIFE HAPPENS
Walking with God is a decision.

TERRIE CHAPPELL

First published in 2012 by Striving Together Publications, a
ministry of Lancaster Baptist Church, Lancaster, CA 93535.
Striving Together Publications is committed to providing tried,
trusted, and proven books that will further equip local churches
to carry out the Great Commission. Your comments and
suggestions are valued.

Striving Together Publications
4020 E. Lancaster Blvd.
Lancaster, CA 93535
800.201.7748

Cover design by Andrew Jones
Layout by Craig Parker
Edited by Danielle Mordh and Monica Bass

ISBN 978-1-59894-189-0

Printed in the United States of America

TABLE OF CONTENTS

excellent choices

Key Verses

PHILIPPIANS 1:9–11

9   And this I pray, that your love may abound yet more and more in knowledge and in all judgment;

10   That ye may approve things that are excellent; that ye may be sincere and without offence till the day of Christ;

11   Being filled with the fruits of righteousness, which are by Jesus Christ, unto the glory and praise of God.

Overview

All of us routinely make choices that have a great impact on our own lives and on the lives of others. These choices actually determine our fulfillment in the Christian life and the future of our lives. The best planning begins with the end in mind. So if you desire a vibrant relationship with the Lord and a future of joy and fulfillment, plan for it today by making excellent choices.

Lesson Aim

When we choose obedience to the Word of God and make conscious choices to daily submit our lives to the direction of the Holy Spirit, we are shaping a future for ourselves of unparalleled blessings.

Introduction

_____

_____

_____

I. The Power of _____ Choices

II. The Guides to _____ Choices

A. *God's* _____

JEREMIAH 17:9

9   The heart is deceitful above all things, and desperately wicked: who can know it?

PROVERBS 3:17–18

17   Her ways are ways of pleasantness, and all her paths are peace.
18   She is a tree of life to them that lay hold upon her: and happy is every one that retaineth her.

PHILIPPIANS 1:9–10

9   And this I pray, that your love may abound yet more and more in knowledge and in all judgment;
10   That ye may approve things that are excellent; that ye may be sincere and without offence till the day of Christ.

B. *The Holy* _____

JOHN 16:7

7   Nevertheless I tell you the truth; It is expedient for you that I go away: for if I go not away, the Comforter

will not come unto you; but if I depart, I will send him
unto you.

EPHESIANS 1:13
13 In whom ye also trusted, after that ye heard the
word of truth, the gospel of your salvation: in whom
also after that ye believed, ye were sealed with that
holy Spirit of promise,

JOHN 14:26
26 But the Comforter, which is the Holy Ghost, whom
the Father will send in my name, he shall teach you
all things, and bring all things to your remembrance,
whatsoever I have said unto you.

III. The Future of _____ Choices

A. A _____ walk with God

B. The _____ of God's promises

Conclusion

_____

_____

_____

Study Questions

1. Why are the individual choices we make so important?

2. What two guides has God given us to help us make excellent choices?

3. Why should we be cautious about the advice to "just follow your heart"?

4. What tool does the Holy Spirit use to teach and guide us?

5. As you look back over the past several years, can you identify a choice you made previously that has had a significant influence in your life today?

6. On a scale of 1–10, how would you rate your current walk with God? In what ways would you like to see it improve through the course of this study?

7. A great future starts with the right choices today. What choices do you need to make this week that will be steps in the right direction of a strong walk with God in the future?

8. The lessons in this study outline key areas of choice for women and the Scriptures that relate. Would you be willing to determine from the beginning that you want your choices to be guided by God's Word and the Holy Spirit? If so, write out a prayer to the Lord to solidify that decision:

Memory Verse

PHILIPPIANS 1:10
10 That ye may approve things that are excellent; that ye may be sincere and without offence till the day of Christ.

choose to be real

Key Verses

JOSHUA 24:14–15, 23–27

14 Now therefore fear the LORD, and serve him in sincerity and in truth: and put away the gods which your fathers served on the other side of the flood, and in Egypt; and serve ye the LORD.

15 And if it seem evil unto you to serve the LORD, choose you this day whom ye will serve; whether the gods which your fathers served that were on the other side of the flood, or the gods of the Amorites, in whose land ye dwell: but as for me and my house, we will serve the LORD.

23 Now therefore put away, said he, the strange gods which are among you, and incline your heart unto the LORD God of Israel.

24 And the people said unto Joshua, The LORD our God will we serve, and his voice will we obey.

25 So Joshua made a covenant with the people that day, and set them a statute and an ordinance in Shechem.

26 And Joshua wrote these words in the book of the law of God, and took a great stone, and set it up there under an oak, that was by the sanctuary of the LORD.

27 And Joshua said unto all the people, Behold, this stone shall be a witness unto us; for it hath heard all the words of the LORD which he spake unto us: it shall be therefore a witness unto you, lest ye deny your God.

Overview

The choice of authenticity is foundational for every other choice in the following lessons. If we want to cultivate lives that reach deeper than the external disciplines or visible evidences of Christianity, then at the core of our decisions must be hearts that are authentically hungry for God.

Lesson Aim

Christian authenticity is a treasure. In this lesson, we will understand its characteristics and outline how we choose it. God's Word encourages us to refuse to settle for half-hearted service or surface success. We must determine to genuinely walk with God, and ask Him to, by His grace, work His likeness into our lives.

Introduction

_____

_____

_____

I. The _____ of a Real Christian

2 TIMOTHY 1:5

5   When I call to remembrance the unfeigned faith that is
in thee, which dwelt first in thy grandmother Lois, and thy
mother Eunice; and I am persuaded that in thee also.

    A. The _____ of authenticity

    B. A _____ of authenticity

II. _____ of a Real Christian

    A. _____ living

ACTS 4:34–35

34 Neither was there any among them that lacked:
for as many as were possessors of lands or houses
sold them, and brought the prices of the things that
were sold,

35 And laid them down at the apostles' feet: and
distribution was made unto every man according as
he had need.

ACTS 5:1–10

1   But a certain man named Ananias, with Sapphira
his wife, sold a possession,

2   And kept back part of the price, his wife also being privy to it, and brought a certain part, and laid it at the apostles' feet.

3   But Peter said, Ananias, why hath Satan filled thine heart to lie to the Holy Ghost, and to keep back part of the price of the land?

4   Whiles it remained, was it not thine own? and after it was sold, was it not in thine own power? why hast thou conceived this thing in thine heart? thou hast not lied unto men, but unto God.

5   And Ananias hearing these words fell down, and gave up the ghost: and great fear came on all them that heard these things.

6   And the young men arose, wound him up, and carried him out, and buried him.

7   And it was about the space of three hours after, when his wife, not knowing what was done, came in.

8   And Peter answered unto her, Tell me whether ye sold the land for so much? And she said, Yea, for so much.

9   Then Peter said unto her, How is it that ye have agreed together to tempt the Spirit of the Lord? behold, the feet of them which have buried thy husband are at the door, and shall carry thee out.

10   Then fell she down straightway at his feet, and yielded up the ghost: and the young men came in, and found her dead, and, carrying her forth, buried her by her husband.

1 SAMUEL 15:22

22   And Samuel said, Hath the LORD as great delight in burnt offerings and sacrifices, as in obeying the voice of the LORD? Behold, to obey is better than sacrifice, and to hearken than the fat of rams.

1 JOHN 1:8–9

8   *If we say that we have no sin, we deceive ourselves, and the truth is not in us.*

9   *If we confess our sins, he is faithful and just to forgive us our sins, and to cleanse us from all unrighteousness.*

B.   _____ *for souls*

MARK 16:15

15   *...Go ye into all the world, and preach the gospel to every creature.*

JUDE 22

22   *And of some have compassion, making a difference.*

C.   _____ *walk*

JOHN 15:1–8

1   *I am the true vine, and my Father is the husbandman.*

2   *Every branch in me that beareth not fruit he taketh away: and every branch that beareth fruit, he purgeth it, that it may bring forth more fruit.*

3   *Now ye are clean through the word which I have spoken unto you.*

4   *Abide in me, and I in you. As the branch cannot bear fruit of itself, except it abide in the vine; no more can ye, except ye abide in me.*

5   *I am the vine, ye are the branches: He that abideth in me, and I in him, the same bringeth forth much fruit: for without me ye can do nothing.*

6   *If a man abide not in me, he is cast forth as a branch, and is withered; and men gather them, and cast them into the fire, and they are burned.*

7   If ye abide in me, and my words abide in you, ye shall ask what ye will, and it shall be done unto you.
8   Herein is my Father glorified, that ye bear much fruit; so shall ye be my disciples.

GALATIANS 2:20
20   I am crucified with Christ: nevertheless I live; yet not I, but Christ liveth in me: and the life which I now live in the flesh I live by the faith of the Son of God, who loved me, and gave himself for me.

PHILIPPIANS 2:13
13   For it is God which worketh in you both to will and to do of his good pleasure.

D.   _____ *spirit*

JOHN 13:35
35   By this shall all men know that ye are my disciples, if ye have love one to another."

JOHN 13:34
34   A new commandment I give unto you, That ye love one another; as I have loved you, that ye also love one another.

JOHN 15:12
12   This is my commandment, That ye love one another, as I have loved you.

JOHN 15:17
17   These things I command you, that ye love one another.

1 JOHN 4:8
8   He that loveth not knoweth not God; for God is love.

III. How to _____ a Real Christian

JOSHUA 24:14

14 Now therefore fear the LORD, and serve him in sincerity and in truth: and put away the gods which your fathers served on the other side of the flood, and in Egypt; and serve ye the LORD.

A. Make a _____.

JOSHUA 24:15

15 And if it seem evil unto you to serve the LORD, choose you this day whom ye will serve; whether the gods which your fathers served that were on the other side of the flood, or the gods of the Amorites, in whose land ye dwell: but as for me and my house, we will serve the LORD.

B. Make a _____.

JOSHUA 24:23

23 Now therefore put away, said he, the strange gods which are among you, and incline your heart unto the LORD God of Israel.

C. Make a commemorative _____.

JOSHUA 24:26–27

26 And Joshua wrote these words in the book of the law of God, and took a great stone, and set it up there under an oak, that was by the sanctuary of the LORD. 27 And Joshua said unto all the people, Behold, this stone shall be a witness unto us; for it hath heard all the words of the LORD which he spake unto us: it shall be therefore a witness unto you, lest ye deny your God.

Conclusion

Study Questions

1. Why is the choice of authenticity foundational for the other choices in our study?

2. List the four "marks of a real Christian" given in this lesson.

3. What does 1 Samuel 15:22 give as an indicator of our genuineness toward the Lord?

4. What three steps to authenticity do we learn from Joshua's instruction to Israel?

5. Authenticity is not the same as perfection. It simply speaks of a life that is real with God and growing in His grace. As you look back over the past six months, can you see areas of genuine growth in your life? What are they?

6. Joshua instructed the people to make a choice of loyalty. Has there been a time in your life when you have made the decision to completely consecrate your

life to God—to make a choice to authentically live for Him? If so, describe what brought you to that decision.

7. Of the four marks of a real Christian given in this lesson, which one do you see most absent in your life? What steps of action do you need to take to change in that area?

8. What "commemorative memorial(s)" do you have in your life that reminds you of your commitment to God? Or what type of reminder could you find this week?

Memory Verse
JOSHUA 24:14A
14 Now therefore fear the LORD, and serve him in sincerity and in truth...

choose to live by faith

Key Verses

EXODUS 2:1–9

1 And there went a man of the house of Levi, and took to wife a daughter of Levi.

2 And the woman conceived, and bare a son: and when she saw him that he was a goodly child, she hid him three months.

3 And when she could not longer hide him, she took for him an ark of bulrushes, and daubed it with slime and with pitch, and put the child therein; and she laid it in the flags by the river's brink.

4 And his sister stood afar off, to wit what would be done to him.

5 And the daughter of Pharaoh came down to wash herself at the river; and her maidens walked along by the river's side; and when she saw the ark among the flags, she sent her maid to fetch it.

6 And when she had opened it, she saw the child: and, behold, the babe wept. And she had compassion on him, and said, This is one of the Hebrews' children.

7 Then said his sister to Pharaoh's daughter, Shall I go and call to thee a nurse of the Hebrew women, that she may nurse the child for thee?

8 And Pharaoh's daughter said to her, Go. And the maid went and called the child's mother.

9 And Pharaoh's daughter said unto her, Take this child away, and nurse it for me, and I will give thee thy wages. And the woman took the child, and nursed it.

Overview

As ladies, we try so desperately to control our circumstances and change the people around us. In reality, we can do neither. It's much wiser and far better to choose to draw close to our God and trust Him. He is the only one who can change our lives and shape our futures.

Lesson Aim

Faith in God is the foundation of the Christian life. Through this lesson, we learn how to choose and exercise faith. When we choose to honor God by our faith, we have the privilege of seeing God intervene and reward our faith in ways we could have never manipulated.

Introduction

_____

_____

_____

EXODUS 1:13–14
13 *And the Egyptians made the children of Israel to serve with rigour:*
14 *And they made their lives bitter with hard bondage, in morter, and in brick, and in all manner of service in the field: all their service, wherein they made them serve, was with rigour.*

EXODUS 1:15–16
15 *And the king of Egypt spake to the Hebrew midwives, of which the name of the one was Shiphrah, and the name of the other Puah:*
16 *And he said, When ye do the office of a midwife to the Hebrew women, and see them upon the stools; if it be a son, then ye shall kill him: but if it be a daughter, then she shall live.*

I. _____ by Faith

HEBREWS 11:23
23 *By faith Moses, when he was born, was hid three months of his parents* [Jochebed and Amram], *because they saw he was a proper child; and they were not afraid of the king's commandment.*

    A. *Faith is a* _____.

EPHESIANS 2:8–9

8   For by grace are ye saved through faith; and that not of yourselves: it is the gift of God:

9   Not of works, lest any man should boast.

HEBREWS 11:6

6   But without faith it is impossible to please him: for he that cometh to God must believe that he is, and that he is a rewarder of them that diligently seek him.

B. Faith is a _____.

ROMANS 8:28

28   And we know that all things work together for good to them that love God, to them who are the called according to his purpose.

II. _____ Faith

PSALM 9:10

10   And they that know thy name will put their trust in thee: for thou, LORD, hast not forsaken them that seek thee.

A. _____ your Bible.

ROMANS 10:17

17   So then faith cometh by hearing, and hearing by the word of God.

B. _____ church.

HEBREWS 13:7

7   Remember them which have the rule over you, who have spoken unto you the word of God: whose faith follow, considering the end of their conversation.

C. _____.

III. _____ Faith

JAMES 2:20

20 But wilt thou know, O vain man, that faith without works is dead?

A. Use your faith though it be _____.

MATTHEW 17:20

20 …verily I say unto you, If ye have faith as a grain of mustard seed, ye shall say unto this mountain, Remove hence to yonder place; and it shall remove; and nothing shall be impossible unto you.

B. Use your faith though it be _____.

IV. _____ God

EXODUS 2:3

3 And when she could not longer hide him, she took for him an ark of bulrushes, and daubed it with slime and with pitch, and put the child therein; and she laid it in the flags by the river's brink.

PROVERBS 3:5–6

5 Trust in the LORD with all thine heart; and lean not unto thine own understanding.
6 In all thy ways acknowledge him, and he shall direct thy paths.

A. Remember the _____.

1 SAMUEL 17:37

37 David said moreover, The LORD that delivered me out of the paw of the lion, and out of the paw of the bear, he will deliver me out of the hand of this Philistine. And Saul said unto David, Go, and the LORD be with thee.

B. Remember the _____.

GENESIS 18:10

10 And he said, I will certainly return unto thee according to the time of life; and, lo, Sarah thy wife shall have a son. And Sarah heard it in the tent door, which was behind him.

ROMANS 4:20

20 He staggered not at the promise of God through unbelief; but was strong in faith, giving glory to God;

Conclusion

EXODUS 2:8–9

8 And Pharaoh's daughter said to her, Go. And the maid went and called the child's mother.

9 And Pharaoh's daughter said unto her, Take this child away, and nurse it for me, and I will give thee thy wages. And the woman took the child, and nursed it.

HEBREWS 11:24–26

24 By faith Moses, when he was come to years, refused to be called the son of Pharaoh's daughter;

25 Choosing rather to suffer affliction with the people of God, than to enjoy the pleasures of sin for a season;

26 *Esteeming the reproach of Christ greater riches than the treasures in Egypt: for he had respect unto the recompence of the reward.*

_____

_____

_____

Study Questions

1. What woman's life did we study throughout this chapter to understand faith?

2. What chapter in the New Testament lists heroes of faith?

3. What are the three ways given in this lesson to nurture and grow your faith?

4. What two particular areas will help our faith grow if we choose to remember them?

5. The Christian life is a journey of faith. Describe an area in which God has increased your faith in the past six months.

6. Our tendency in trouble is to attempt to control our circumstances or the people around us. Why is this futile? And what is a wiser response?

7.   In what ways are you nurturing your faith? In what ways could you be more diligent?

8.   List two or three promises from God's Word that have been a help to your faith in recent circumstances.

Memory Verses

PROVERBS 3:5–6

5   *Trust in the LORD with all thine heart; and lean not unto thine own understanding.*

6   *In all thy ways acknowledge him, and he shall direct thy paths.*

choose to listen to God

Key Verses

MATTHEW 5:6
6 Blessed are they which do hunger and thirst after righteousness: for they shall be filled.

1 PETER 2:2
2 As newborn babes, desire the sincere milk of the word, that ye may grow thereby.

Overview

The choice to walk with God boils down to one word: appetite. Just as we choose physical food based on what we desire, so we choose our spiritual food based on our appetite for the Lord. If we want to be spiritually strong, we must train our spiritual appetites for the Lord. In this lesson, we learn how to change our appetites, and we examine four disciplines that will help us maintain a faithful walk with God.

Lesson Aim

Those in Scripture who were greatly used by God had a close walk with God. They hungered for God with intensity and focus. As Christian women, we, too, must develop a true hunger for God and His Word.

Introduction

_____

_____

_____

JAMES 4:8
8   Draw nigh to God, and he will draw nigh to you....

I.   Training Your _____

MATTHEW 5:6
6   Blessed are they which do hunger and thirst after righteousness: for they shall be filled.

PSALM 84:1–2
1   How amiable are thy tabernacles, O LORD of hosts!
2   My soul longeth, yea, even fainteth for the courts of the LORD: my heart and my flesh crieth out for the living God.

A.   _____

1 PETER 2:2
2   As newborn babes, desire the sincere milk of the word, that ye may grow thereby.

PSALM 119:10
10   With my whole heart have I sought thee: O let me not wander from thy commandments.

PSALM 27:4
4   One thing have I desired of the LORD, that will I seek after; that I may dwell in the house of the LORD all the days of my life, to behold the beauty of the LORD, and to enquire in his temple.

PSALM 63:1

*1   O God, thou art my God; early will I seek thee:
my soul thirsteth for thee, my flesh longeth for thee in
a dry and thirsty land, where no water is;*

PSALM 84:2

*2   My soul longeth, yea, even fainteth for the courts
of the LORD: my heart and my flesh crieth out for the
living God.*

JOHN 6:35

*35   And Jesus said unto them, I am the bread of life:
he that cometh to me shall never hunger; and he that
believeth on me shall never thirst.*

B. _____

1 PETER 2:11

*11   Dearly beloved, I beseech you as strangers and
pilgrims, abstain from fleshly lusts, which war against
the soul.*

PSALM 73:25

*25   Whom have I in heaven but thee? and there is
none upon earth that I desire beside thee.*

C. _____

II. Clarifying Your _____

GENESIS 19:27

*27 And Abraham gat up early in the morning to the place
where he stood before the LORD:*

GENESIS 22:3

3   And Abraham rose up early in the morning, and saddled his ass, and took two of his young men with him, and Isaac his son, and clave the wood for the burnt offering, and rose up, and went unto the place of which God had told him.

EXODUS 24:4

4   And Moses wrote all the words of the LORD, and rose up early in the morning, and builded an altar under the hill, and twelve pillars, according to the twelve tribes of Israel.

EXODUS 34:4

4   And he hewed two tables of stone like unto the first; and Moses rose up early in the morning, and went up unto mount Sinai, as the LORD had commanded him, and took in his hand the two tables of stone.

PSALM 57:8

8   Awake up, my glory; awake, psaltery and harp: I myself will awake early.

PSALM 63:1

1   O God, thou art my God; early will I seek thee…

PSALM 108:2

2   Awake, psaltery and harp: I myself will awake early.

MARK 1:35

35   And in the morning, rising up a great while before day, he went out, and departed into a solitary place, and there prayed.

PROVERBS 8:17

17   I love them that love me; and those that seek me early shall find me.

III. Developing New _____

A. _____

B. _____

C. _____ *journal*

D. _____ *group*

HEBREWS 10:25

25 Not forsaking the assembling of ourselves together, as the manner of some is; but exhorting one another: and so much the more, as ye see the day approaching.

Conclusion

_____

_____

_____

Study Questions

1. The choice to walk with God boils down to one word. What is it?

2. What three steps are given in this lesson to change your spiritual appetites?

3. What four disciplines for a growing walk with God are given in this lesson?

4. Walking with God and spending time in His Word is not merely a system. What is the larger goal?

5. On a scale of 1–10, how strong would you say your spiritual appetites are? Through this lesson, did the Holy Spirit convict you of any competing appetites that you need to eliminate?

6. What is your current Bible reading plan? Or what plan could you begin tomorrow?

7. Do you need to find an accountability partner in your church to encourage you in your walk with the Lord? If so, write down the name of a mature Christian lady that you plan this week to ask for accountability.

8. Through what verses in your Bible reading has the Lord recently spoken to your heart? Write down the references and how He spoke to you, and then plan to share them with another Christian lady for mutual encouragement.

Memory Verse

MATTHEW 5:6

6 Blessed are they which do hunger and thirst after righteousness: for they shall be filled.

choose to talk to God

Key Verses

JEREMIAH 33:3

3   *Call unto me, and I will answer thee, and shew thee great and mighty things, which thou knowest not.*

Overview

Prayer is one of the most incredible resources at our disposal. Through prayer, we have direct access to our Heavenly Father. We share our hearts with Him and seek His resources to meet our needs. And yet, as valuable as prayer is, it is one of the most neglected resources. In this lesson, we learn to regularly choose to commune with the Lord.

Lesson Aim

Statistics say that prayer is the most often talked about and the least practiced discipline in the Christian life. In this lesson, we learn how we can move beyond mere talk of prayer and become true women of prayer.

Introduction

_____

_____

_____

JEREMIAH 33:3
3   *Call unto me, and I will answer thee, and shew thee great and mighty things, which thou knowest not.*

1 SAMUEL 1:27
27   *For this child I prayed; and the LORD hath given me my petition which I asked of him.*

I.   _____

A. *Commit to _____.*

LUKE 18:1
1   *And he spake a parable unto them to this end, that men ought always to pray, and not to faint;*

1 CHRONICLES 16:11
11   *Seek the LORD and his strength, seek his face continually.*

1 THESSALONIANS 5:17
17   *Pray without ceasing.*

DANIEL 6:10
10   *Now when Daniel knew that the writing was signed, he went into his house; and his windows being open in his chamber toward Jerusalem, he kneeled upon his knees three times a day, and prayed, and gave thanks before his God, as he did aforetime.*

B. Commit to a _____.

JOHN 18:2

2   And Judas also, which betrayed him, knew the place: for Jesus ofttimes resorted thither with his disciples.

PSALM 5:3

3   My voice shalt thou hear in the morning, O LORD; in the morning will I direct my prayer unto thee, and will look up.

MARK 1:35

35   And in the morning, rising up a great while before day, he went out, and departed into a solitary place, and there prayed.

PSALM 4:8

8   I will both lay me down in peace, and sleep: for thou, LORD, only makest me dwell in safety.

PSALM 55:17

17   Evening, and morning, and at noon, will I pray, and cry aloud: and he shall hear my voice.

LUKE 24:30

30   And it came to pass, as he sat at meat with them, he took bread, and blessed it, and brake, and gave to them.

PSALM 116:2

2   Because he hath inclined his ear unto me, therefore will I call upon him as long as I live.

MATTHEW 6:6

6   But thou, when thou prayest, enter into thy closet, and when thou hast shut thy door, pray to thy Father

which is in secret; and thy Father which seeth in secret shall reward thee openly.

MATTHEW 18:19
19   Again I say unto you, That if two of you shall agree on earth as touching any thing that they shall ask, it shall be done for them of my Father which is in heaven.

ACTS 10:9
9   On the morrow, as they went on their journey, and drew nigh unto the city, Peter went up upon the housetop to pray about the sixth hour:

II. _____

PSALM 66:18
18   If I regard iniquity in my heart, the Lord will not hear me.

ISAIAH 59:1–2
1   Behold, the LORD's hand is not shortened, that it cannot save; neither his ear heavy, that it cannot hear:
2   But your iniquities have separated between you and your God, and your sins have hid his face from you, that he will not hear.

MARK 11:25–26
25   And when ye stand praying, forgive, if ye have ought against any: that your Father also which is in heaven may forgive you your trespasses.
26   But if ye do not forgive, neither will your Father which is in heaven forgive your trespasses.

1 PETER 3:7

7   Likewise, ye husbands, dwell with them according to knowledge, giving honour unto the wife, as unto the weaker vessel, and as being heirs together of the grace of life; that your prayers be not hindered.

PSALM 139:23–24

23   Search me, O God, and know my heart: try me, and know my thoughts:
24   And see if there be any wicked way in me, and lead me in the way everlasting.

1 JOHN 1:9

9   If we confess our sins, he is faithful and just to forgive us our sins, and to cleanse us from all unrighteousness.

III. _____

1 SAMUEL 1:10

10   And she was in bitterness of soul, and prayed unto the LORD, and wept sore.

1 SAMUEL 1:15

15   And Hannah answered and said, No, my lord, I am a woman of a sorrowful spirit: I have drunk neither wine nor strong drink, but have poured out my soul before the LORD.

A. *Pray in* _____.

MATTHEW 6:6

6   But thou, when thou prayest, enter into thy closet, and when thou hast shut thy door, pray to thy Father which is in secret; and thy Father which seeth in secret shall reward thee openly.

JAMES 4:2

2   ...ye have not, because ye ask not.

1 PETER 5:7

7   Casting all your care upon him; for he careth for you.

B. Pray _____.

MATTHEW 6:7

7   But when ye pray, use not vain repetitions, as the heathen do: for they think that they shall be heard for their much speaking.

C. Pray _____.

D. Keep a _____.

IV. _____

Conclusion

_____

_____

_____

Study Questions

1. What woman in Scripture did we look at in this lesson who brought her pain and rejection to the Lord and saw God answer her prayer?

2. Who prayed three times every day with such consistency that even his enemies could count on his faithfulness?

3. What times in Scripture are mentioned as times for prayer?

4. Which two sins mentioned in this lesson are specifically mentioned in Scripture as hindrances to prayer?

5. When was the last time that you asked the Lord to thoroughly search your heart? What two Scripture passages are suggested in this lesson as prayers for this process?

6. Where is your "prayer closet" where you regularly go to spend time in prayer? If you are not already in this habit, what place could you make your "prayer closet" as you begin to develop a prayer life?

7.   List some recent answers to prayer that you have seen in the past thirty days.

8.   In addition to seeing God answer your needs through prayer, have you seen God change *you* through the process of seeking Him in prayer? In what ways?

Memory Verse

JEREMIAH 33:3
3   *Call unto me, and I will answer thee, and shew thee great and mighty things, which thou knowest not.*

choose to let go

Key Verses

PHILIPPIANS 3:13–14

13 *Brethren, I count not myself to have apprehended: but this one thing I do, forgetting those things which are behind, and reaching forth unto those things which are before,*
14 *I press toward the mark for the prize of the high calling of God in Christ Jesus.*

Overview

As ladies, we so easily allow our circumstances and other people (or even our *perception* of what others think) to define who we are. A proper perspective only comes when we choose to define ourselves by what God says is true. In this lesson, we learn how God teaches us to view our past and how He can use it to make us trophies of His grace.

Lesson Aim

Many ladies struggle with guilt and pain from their past—baggage that is real and heavy. Yet, God gives us the resources to release the past and press forward into the future—all by the power of grace.

THE CHOICE IS YOURS

Introduction

_____

_____

_____

I. _____

ACTS 8:3

3   As for Saul, he made havock of the church, entering into every house, and haling men and women committed them to prison.

ACTS 22:4–5

4   And I persecuted this way unto the death, binding and delivering into prisons both men and women.

5   As also the high priest doth bear me witness, and all the estate of the elders: from whom also I received letters unto the brethren, and went to Damascus, to bring them which were there bound unto Jerusalem, for to be punished.

ACTS 9:26

26   And when Saul was come to Jerusalem, he assayed to join himself to the disciples: but they were all afraid of him, and believed not that he was a disciple.

PHILIPPIANS 3:13–14

13   Brethren, I count not myself to have apprehended: but this one thing I do, forgetting those things which are behind, and reaching forth unto those things which are before,

14   I press toward the mark for the prize of the high calling of God in Christ Jesus.

II. Dealing with the _____

REVELATION 12:10

10 *And I heard a loud voice saying in heaven, Now is come salvation, and strength, and the kingdom of our God, and the power of his Christ: for the accuser of our brethren is cast down, which accused them before our God day and night.*

PSALM 103:12

12 *As far as the east is from the west, so far hath he removed our transgressions from us.*

HEBREWS 8:12

12 *For I will be merciful to their unrighteousness, and their sins and their iniquities will I remember no more.*

1 JOHN 1:9

9 *If we confess our sins, he is faithful and just to forgive us our sins, and to cleanse us from all unrighteousness.*

III. _____

GENESIS 37:4

4 *And when his brethren saw that their father loved him more than all his brethren, they hated him, and could not speak peaceably unto him.*

GENESIS 37:23–28

23 *And it came to pass, when Joseph was come unto his brethren, that they stript Joseph out of his coat, his coat of many colours that was on him;*
24 *And they took him, and cast him into a pit: and the pit was empty, there was no water in it.*

25   *And they sat down to eat bread: and they lifted up their eyes and looked, and, behold, a company of Ishmeelites came from Gilead with their camels bearing spicery and balm and myrrh, going to carry it down to Egypt.*

26   *And Judah said unto his brethren, What profit is it if we slay our brother, and conceal his blood?*

27   *Come, and let us sell him to the Ishmeelites, and let not our hand be upon him; for he is our brother and our flesh. And his brethren were content.*

28   *Then there passed by Midianites merchantmen; and they drew and lifted up Joseph out of the pit, and sold Joseph to the Ishmeelites for twenty pieces of silver: and they brought Joseph into Egypt.*

GENESIS 41:51

51   *And Joseph called the name of the firstborn Manasseh: For God, said he, hath made me forget all my toil, and all my father's house.*

GENESIS 45:10–11

10   *And thou shalt dwell in the land of Goshen, and thou shalt be near unto me, thou, and thy children, and thy children's children, and thy flocks, and thy herds, and all that thou hast:*

11   *And there will I nourish thee; for yet there are five years of famine; lest thou, and thy household, and all that thou hast, come to poverty.*

GENESIS 50:20

20   *But as for you, ye thought evil against me; but God meant it unto good, to bring to pass, as it is this day, to save much people alive.*

IV. Embracing _____

JUDGES 11:2
2   And Gilead's wife bare him sons; and his wife's sons grew up, and they thrust out Jephthah, and said unto him, Thou shalt not inherit in our father's house; for thou art the son of a strange woman.

JUDGES 11:32
32   So Jephthah passed over unto the children of Ammon to fight against them; and the LORD delivered them into his hands.

HEBREWS 11:31
31   By faith the harlot Rahab perished not with them that believed not, when she had received the spies with peace.

MARK 16:9
9   Now when Jesus was risen early the first day of the week, he appeared first to Mary Magdalene, out of whom he had cast seven devils.

Conclusion

ROMANS 8:28
28   And we know that all things work together for good to them that love God, to them who are the called according to his purpose.

_____

_____

_____

Study Questions

1. Many people define *self-acceptance* by our own perception of ourselves. But what do we use in this lesson to gain a proper perspective?

2. Paul the Apostle had a past that was stained by sin. After receiving God's forgiveness through salvation, what one word summarizes his secret to freeing himself from the grip of the past?

3. Joseph had a painful past brought on by the hatred of others. What did Joseph choose to do to enable him to release himself from the past?

4. God offers us the incredible resource of grace to enable us to forgive. What three Bible characters mentioned in this lesson had troubled pasts but became trophies of grace? Can you think of any others?

5. Who does Scripture call "the accuser"? And what verses are given in this lesson that tell the truth of God's forgiveness? Can you think of other verses to add?

6. What godly Christian do you look up to who had a sinful or painful past? How have you seen God's grace magnified in his or her life?

7. Has there been a sinful or painful area in your past in which you have seen God's grace sever the chains of bitterness and guilt and bring healing? Is there an area from your past that the Holy Spirit brought to mind in this lesson that still needs the touch of God's grace as you choose to release it and forgive?

8. In what ways have you already seen God fulfill the promise of Romans 8:28 in your life? What areas are you still waiting to see Him work all things together for good?

Memory Verses

PHILIPPIANS 3:13–14

13 *Brethren, I count not myself to have apprehended: but this one thing I do, forgetting those things which are behind, and reaching forth unto those things which are before,*

14 *I press toward the mark for the prize of the high calling of God in Christ Jesus.*

choose to press on

Key Verses
PHILIPPIANS 3:13–14
13 *Brethren, I count not myself to have apprehended: but this one thing I do, forgetting those things which are behind, and reaching forth unto those things which are before,*
14 *I press toward the mark for the prize of the high calling of God in Christ Jesus.*

Overview
In our previous lesson, we identified our need to see our past from God's perspective. In this chapter, we explore what God says is true concerning our present and our future potential. And we learn how His truth enables us to press on in spiritual victory.

Lesson Aim
That God would choose to bestow His love on us and that He would create a plan for our lives is a truth beyond comprehension. We can respond to His love by choosing to release our past to Him, accept the unchangeable areas of our present, and yield to His work of transforming us into His image. With His help, we can press on for His glory.

Introduction

_____

_____

_____

I. Our _____

PSALM 139:13–16

13 *For thou hast possessed my reins: thou hast covered me in my mother's womb.*

14 *I will praise thee; for I am fearfully and wonderfully made: marvellous are thy works; and that my soul knoweth right well.*

15 *My substance was not hid from thee, when I was made in secret, and curiously wrought in the lowest parts of the earth.*

16 *Thine eyes did see my substance, yet being unperfect; and in thy book all my members were written, which in continuance were fashioned, when as yet there was none of them.*

II. Our _____

EPHESIANS 1:6

6 *To the praise of the glory of his grace, wherein he hath made us accepted in the beloved.*

III. Our _____

2 CORINTHIANS 10:12

12 *For we dare not make ourselves of the number, or compare ourselves with some that commend themselves: but they measuring themselves by themselves, and comparing themselves among themselves, are not wise.*

A. Attained _____

ROMANS 8:38–39

38 For I am persuaded, that neither death, nor life, nor angels, nor principalities, nor powers, nor things present, nor things to come,

39 Nor height, nor depth, nor any other creature, shall be able to separate us from the love of God, which is in Christ Jesus our Lord.

B. Assault on our _____

IV. Our _____

LUKE 1:37

37 For with God nothing shall be impossible.

A. Ask for God's _____

JOHN 15:5

5 I am the vine, ye are the branches: He that abideth in me, and I in him, the same bringeth forth much fruit: for without me ye can do nothing.

JEREMIAH 33:3

3 Call unto me, and I will answer thee, and shew thee great and mighty things, which thou knowest not.

B. Accurately measure _____ by the Bible

LUKE 13:11–13

11 And, behold, there was a woman which had a spirit of infirmity eighteen years, and was bowed together, and could in no wise lift up herself.

12 *And when Jesus saw her, he called her to him, and said unto her, Woman, thou art loosed from thine infirmity.*
13 *And he laid his hands on her: and immediately she was made straight, and glorified God.*

C. *Apply God's* _____

Conclusion

- God created me, and even before I was born God supervised my total development (Psalm 139).
- God is presently working in me to make me like Christ (Romans 8:28–30).
- I will be patient with myself. God has entrusted me with the potential, gifts, talents, and personality to do His perfect will (Philippians 1:6).
- I will trust that God will continue to equip me to do His will (Philippians 2:13). Whom God calls, He qualifies.
- I will set out to improve the changeable areas as God gives me insight and power (Philippians 4:13). I will seek to fulfill my potential by setting goals for myself.
- I will not use my background or lack of abilities as an excuse for sin or lack of progress in my life (Philippians 3:13–14).
- I will daily confess and forsake sin and seek cleansing through the Word (1 John 1:9).
- I will accept myself as a special person created to fulfill a unique purpose (Psalm 139:14–16). I will

believe God's estimate of me. He loved me enough to send His dearest treasure, Jesus, to die for me (John 3:16). This act alone is a statement that God believes I'm a worthwhile person.

- I will reach out to other people, remembering that they, too, are special and worthy of love (Philippians 2:3–4).
- I will remember it is not *who* I am but *whose* I am that determines my value (Ephesians 2:10).

_____

_____

_____

Study Questions

1. What four areas are given in this lesson in which we need to choose to press on?

2. What three Bible characters are mentioned in this lesson who had some kind of "defect" that made them dependent upon God's grace?

3. Is there something about your person—your appearance—that you have wished you could change, but now see that you need to trust to the Lord? Have you already seen how God has specially used, for His glory, a feature or "handicap" that you would have created differently?

4. What verse teaches us that we do not need to *earn* God's acceptance, but are simply accepted by our position in Christ?

5. All of us tend to look for acceptance based on what we do instead of on God's love. In what areas do you most notice this tendency in yourself?

6. Is there a task the Lord has clearly given you to do that you are experiencing the joy of obedience in performing?

7. What verse teaches us that there is *always* hope for change in our lives with Christ's help?

8. The conclusion to this lesson listed ten statements affirming the truths we studied in this lesson. Which three truths and their corresponding Scripture verses do you most need to focus on this week?

Memory Verses

PHILIPPIANS 3:13–14

13 *Brethren, I count not myself to have apprehended: but this one thing I do, forgetting those things which are behind, and reaching forth unto those things which are before,*

14 *I press toward the mark for the prize of the high calling of God in Christ Jesus.*

choose to be joyful

Key Verses

JOHN 15:11

11   *These things have I spoken unto you, that my joy might remain in you, and that your joy might be full.*

PHILIPPIANS 4:8

8   *Finally, brethren, whatsoever things are true, whatsoever things are honest, whatsoever things are just, whatsoever things are pure, whatsoever things are lovely, whatsoever things are of good report; if there be any virtue, and if there be any praise, think on these things.*

Overview

Our circumstances are constantly changing; yet, Christ desires to give us full and constant joy. This is only possible, however, as we deliberately choose joy. Circumstances change and feelings fluctuate, but the mind that is stayed on Christ can know continual joy. To rejoice is a choice!

Lesson Aim

Everyone who has trusted Christ has the privilege of experiencing full joy. Yet, so few Christians take advantage of this privilege. Why are so many Christians unhappy, disappointed, and miserable, when they could be experiencing Christian joy? In this lesson, we discover how we can choose joy regardless of the circumstances as well as seven reasons we can continually rejoice.

Introduction

_____

_____

_____

DEUTERONOMY 11:11

11   *But the land…is a land of hills and valleys….*

1 KINGS 20:28

28   *And there came a man of God, and spake unto the king of Israel, and said, Thus saith the* LORD, *Because the Syrians have said, The* LORD *is God of the hills, but he is not God of the valleys, therefore will I deliver all this great multitude into thine hand, and ye shall know that I am the* LORD.

PSALM 46:1

1   *God is our refuge and strength, a very present help in trouble.*

PSALM 16:11

11   *Thou wilt shew me the path of life: in thy presence is fulness of joy; at thy right hand there are pleasures for evermore.*

JOHN 15:11

11   *These things have I spoken unto you, that my joy might remain in you, and that your joy might be full.*

I.   The _____ of Joy

JOHN 16:22

22   *…your joy no man taketh from you.*

JOHN 17:13

13 *And now come I to thee; and these things I speak in the world, that they might have my joy fulfilled in themselves.*

II. A _____ for Joy

PHILIPPIANS 1:25

25 *And having this confidence, I know that I shall abide and continue with you all for your furtherance and joy of faith;*

PHILIPPIANS 2:17

17 *Yea, and if I be offered upon the sacrifice and service of your faith, I joy, and rejoice with you all.*

A. _____ *the secret*

PHILIPPIANS 4:8

8 *Finally, brethren, whatsoever things are true, whatsoever things are honest, whatsoever things are just, whatsoever things are pure, whatsoever things are lovely, whatsoever things are of good report; if there be any virtue, and if there be any praise, think on these things.*

B. _____ *a single mind*

PHILIPPIANS 1:13

13 *So that my bonds in Christ are manifest in all the palace, and in all other places;*

PHILIPPIANS 1:17

17 *... knowing that I am set for the defence of the gospel.*

PHILIPPIANS 1:12

12 But I would ye should understand, brethren, that the things which happened unto me have fallen out rather unto the furtherance of the gospel;

III. _____ for Joy

A. Personal _____ with Christ

PHILIPPIANS 1:1

1 Paul and Timotheus, the servants of Jesus Christ, to all the saints in Christ Jesus which are at Philippi...

JOHN 17:3

3 And this is life eternal, that they might know thee the only true God, and Jesus Christ, whom thou hast sent.

PSALM 21:1

1 The king shall joy in thy strength, O LORD; and in thy salvation how greatly shall he rejoice!

PSALM 9:14

14 ...I will rejoice in thy salvation.

PSALM 51:12

12 Restore unto me the joy of thy salvation; and uphold me with thy free spirit.

HABAKKUK 3:17–18

17 Although the fig tree shall not blossom, neither shall fruit be in the vines; the labour of the olive shall fail, and the fields shall yield no meat; the flock shall be cut off from the fold, and there shall be no herd in the stalls:

18 Yet I will rejoice in the LORD, I will joy in the God of my salvation.

B. Position as _____

PHILIPPIANS 1:1

1 Paul and Timotheus, the servants of Jesus Christ…

ACTS 20:24

24 But none of these things move me, neither count I my life dear unto myself, so that I might finish my course with joy, and the ministry, which I have received of the Lord Jesus, to testify the gospel of the grace of God.

MATTHEW 25:21

21 …Well done, thou good and faithful servant: thou hast been faithful over a few things, I will make thee ruler over many things: enter thou into the joy of thy lord.

C. Pleasant _____ of people

PHILIPPIANS 1:3–5

3 I thank my God upon every remembrance of you,
4 Always in every prayer of mine for you all making request with joy,
5 For your fellowship in the gospel from the first day until now.

D. Perfect _____ in God's plan

PHILIPPIANS 1:20

20 According to my earnest expectation and my hope, that in nothing I shall be ashamed, but that with all boldness, as always, so now also Christ shall

*be magnified in my body, whether it be by life, or
by death.*

PHILIPPIANS 1:6

*6 Being confident of this very thing, that he which
hath begun a good work in you will perform it until
the day of Jesus Christ:*

PROVERBS 3:5–6

*5 Trust in the LORD with all thine heart; and lean
not unto thine own understanding.*
*6 In all thy ways acknowledge him, and he shall
direct thy paths.*

E. *Precious* _____

PHILIPPIANS 1:7–8

*7 ...I have you in my heart; inasmuch as both in
my bonds, and in the defence and confirmation of the
gospel, ye all are partakers of my grace.*
*8 For God is my record, how greatly I long after you
all in the bowels of Jesus Christ.*

F. *Pioneers of the* _____

ROMANS 1:15

*15 So, as much as in me is, I am ready to preach the
gospel to you that are at Rome also.*

PHILIPPIANS 1:12

*12 But I would ye should understand, brethren, that
the things which happened unto me have fallen out
rather unto the furtherance of the gospel.*

LUKE 15:10

10 Likewise, I say unto you, there is joy in the presence of the angels of God over one sinner that repenteth.

G. *Privilege of seeing Christ* _____

PHILIPPIANS 1:20–21

20 According to my earnest expectation and my hope, that in nothing I shall be ashamed, but that with all boldness, as always, so now also Christ shall be magnified in my body, whether it be by life, or by death.

21 For to me to live is Christ, and to die is gain.

Conclusion

_____

_____

_____

Study Questions

1. What is the privilege that every child of God has, yet so few take advantage of?

2. What is the number one thief of joy?

3. What is the difference between happiness and joy?

4. What is the secret of Christian joy?

5. Is there a reoccurring situation or burden that continually attempts to steal your joy? What truths from Philippians 1 could you have ready to meditate on and rejoice in next time that situation arises?

6. One of the best reasons Christians have for rejoicing is our relationship with Christ. Describe when you trusted Christ as your Saviour, and write down several attributes of Christ in which you can rejoice.

7. Have you ever wondered why God put you in a circumstance, place, or position that you would never have chosen for yourself, and then later realized it was so someone could be saved? If so, describe that situation.

8. As a general rule, would you say that you are more of a thermometer or a thermostat for those around you—at home, work, church, school?

Memory Verses

JOHN 15:11

11 These things have I spoken unto you, that my joy might remain in you, and that your joy might be full.

PHILIPPIANS 4:8

8 Finally, brethren, whatsoever things are true, whatsoever things are honest, whatsoever things are just, whatsoever things are pure, whatsoever things are lovely, whatsoever things are of good report; if there be any virtue, and if there be any praise, think on these things.

choose to be strong

Key Verses

1 PETER 1:6–7

6   Wherein ye greatly rejoice, though now for a season, if need be, ye are in heaviness through manifold temptations:

7   That the trial of your faith, being much more precious than of gold that perisheth, though it be tried with fire, might be found unto praise and honour and glory at the appearing of Jesus Christ:

Overview

The Christian life is not free of trials. In fact, God actually uses the difficult times in our lives to mature our faith and give us greater strength in Him. The Lord uses trials as a furnace to refine us. In the furnace of affliction, God purifies our faith so we can one day present it to the Lord, untarnished and sparkling with His glory.

Lesson Aim

Many ladies who are in the midst of a trial tighten their jaw in resolve and, through gritted teeth, say, "I just have to be strong." Yet, God doesn't call on us to pull strength from ourselves during trials. Trials themselves, in fact, reveal just how small our reserves of strength actually are. God offers to give us His strength through the fire. Choosing strength is simply a matter of choosing to receive the gift of God's strength.

Introduction

_____

_____

_____

1 PETER 1:6–7
6 *Wherein ye greatly rejoice, though now for a season, if need be, ye are in heaviness through manifold temptations:*
7 *That the trial of your faith, being much more precious than of gold that perisheth, though it be tried with fire, might be found unto praise and honour and glory at the appearing of Jesus Christ.*

ISAIAH 41:10
10 *Fear thou not; for I am with thee: be not dismayed; for I am thy God: I will strengthen thee; yea, I will help thee; yea, I will uphold thee with the right hand of my righteousness.*

PSALM 73:26
26 *My flesh and my heart faileth: but God is the strength of my heart, and my portion for ever.*

I.   Bible Truths about _____

1 PETER 1:6–7
6 *Wherein ye greatly rejoice, though now for a season, if need be, ye are in heaviness through manifold temptations:*
7 *That the trial of your faith, being much more precious than of gold that perisheth, though it be tried with fire, might be found unto praise and honour and glory at the appearing of Jesus Christ:*

A. Remember it won't last _____.

PSALM 30:5

5 ...weeping may endure for a night, but joy cometh in the morning.

2 CORINTHIANS 4:17–18

17 For our light affliction, which is but for a moment, worketh for us a far more exceeding and eternal weight of glory;

18 While we look not at the things which are seen, but at the things which are not seen: for the things which are seen are temporal; but the things which are not seen are eternal.

B. Acknowledge the _____ to God.

PSALM 13:1–2A

1 How long wilt thou forget me, O LORD? for ever? how long wilt thou hide thy face from me?

2 How long shall I take counsel in my soul, having sorrow in my heart daily?

PSALM 28:1–2

1 Unto thee will I cry, O LORD my rock; be not silent to me: lest, if thou be silent to me, I become like them that go down into the pit.

2 Hear the voice of my supplications, when I cry unto thee, when I lift up my hands toward thy holy oracle.

PSALM 69:1–3

1 Save me, O God; for the waters are come in unto my soul.

2 I sink in deep mire, where there is no standing: I am come into deep waters, where the floods overflow me.

3   I am weary of my crying: my throat is dried: mine eyes fail while I wait for my God.

PSALM 46:1
1   God is our refuge and strength, a very present help in trouble.

C. Trust the Father's _____.

JOB 1:9–10, 12
9   Then Satan answered the LORD, and said, Doth Job fear God for nought?
10   Hast not thou made an hedge about him, and about his house, and about all that he hath on every side? thou hast blessed the work of his hands, and his substance is increased in the land.
12   And the LORD said unto Satan, Behold, all that he hath is in thy power; only upon himself put not forth thine hand. So Satan went forth from the presence of the LORD.

II. God's Work through _____

A. He _____ us back to Him.

PSALM 119:67
67   Before I was afflicted I went astray: but now have I kept thy word.

B. He _____ us for spiritual growth.

C. He _____ us.

PROVERBS 25:4
4   Take away the dross from the silver, and there shall come forth a vessel for the finer.

MALACHI 3:3

3 *And he shall sit as a refiner and purifier of silver: and he shall purify the sons of Levi, and purge them as gold and silver, that they may offer unto the* LORD *an offering in righteousness.*

HEBREWS 12:10–11

10 *For they verily for a few days chastened us after their own pleasure; but he for our profit, that we might be partakers of his holiness.*

11 *Now no chastening for the present seemeth to be joyous, but grievous: nevertheless afterward it yieldeth the peaceable fruit of righteousness unto them which are exercised thereby.*

D. *He gives us the opportunity to _____ others.*

2 CORINTHIANS 1:4

4 *Who comforteth us in all our tribulation, that we may be able to comfort them which are in any trouble, by the comfort wherewith we ourselves are comforted of God.*

E. *He lets us _____ others to Him.*

DANIEL 3:29

29 *…That every people, nation, and language, which speak any thing amiss against the God of Shadrach, Meshach, and Abednego, shall be cut in pieces, and their houses shall be made a dunghill: because there is no other God that can deliver after this sort.*

III. Our _____ to Trials

2 CORINTHIANS 12:9A

9   *And he said unto me, My grace is sufficient for thee: for my strength is made perfect in weakness.*

2 CORINTHIANS 12:9B–10

9   *Most gladly therefore will I rather glory in my infirmities, that the power of Christ may rest upon me.*

10   *Therefore I take pleasure in infirmities, in reproaches, in necessities, in persecutions, in distresses for Christ's sake: for when I am weak, then am I strong.*

A. *Don't _____.*

RUTH 1:1, 5

1   *Now it came to pass in the days when the judges ruled, that there was a famine in the land. And a certain man of Bethlehemjudah went to sojourn in the country of Moab, he, and his wife, and his two sons.*

5   *And Mahlon and Chilion died also both of them; and the woman was left of her two sons and her husband.*

B. _____ *God's Word.*

PSALM 12:6

6   *The words of the LORD are pure words: as silver tried in a furnace of earth, purified seven times.*

C. _____.

JAMES 1:2–4

2   *My brethren, count it all joy when ye fall into divers temptations;*

3   Knowing this, that the trying of your faith worketh patience.

4   But let patience have her perfect work, that ye may be perfect and entire, wanting nothing.

D. _____ **on the Lord.**

PSALM 27:14

14   Wait on the LORD: be of good courage, and he shall strengthen thine heart: wait, I say, on the LORD.

ROMANS 8:28

28   And we know that all things work together for good to them that love God, to them who are the called according to his purpose.

1 PETER 5:7

7   Casting all your care upon him; for he careth for you.

1 PETER 4:19

19   Wherefore let them that suffer according to the will of God commit the keeping of their souls to him in well doing, as unto a faithful Creator.

ISAIAH 26:3

3   Thou wilt keep him in perfect peace, whose mind is stayed on thee: because he trusteth in thee.

Conclusion

1 PETER 1:7

7   That the trial of your faith, being much more precious than of gold that perisheth, though it be tried with fire, might be found unto praise and honour and glory at the appearing of Jesus Christ.

Study Questions

1. How are our trials like a refining fire for gold?

2. How have you seen God use trials or difficulties in your life to remove impurities?

3. What are the three truths we learn from 1 Peter 1 about trials?

4. What five ways are mentioned in this lesson that God works in our lives through trials?

5. Can you describe a time in which God used a trial in your life to work in one or more of the five ways listed above?

6. What are the four practical ways given in this lesson that we can "choose strength"?

7. It is impossible to continually experience God's strength apart from the Bible. Are you spending time in God's Word daily? What are some recent Scriptures God has used to strengthen your heart?

8. Trials allow us to have something of great value to present to the Lord when we see Him face to face. What is it?

Memory Verses

1 PETER 1:6–7

6 *Wherein ye greatly rejoice, though now for a season, if need be, ye are in heaviness through manifold temptations:*

7 *That the trial of your faith, being much more precious than of gold that perisheth, though it be tried with fire, might be found unto praise and honour and glory at the appearing of Jesus Christ:*

choose to succeed

Key Verses

1 PETER 1:6–7

6 *Wherein ye greatly rejoice, though now for a season, if need be, ye are in heaviness through manifold temptations:*

7 *That the trial of your faith, being much more precious than of gold that perisheth, though it be tried with fire, might be found unto praise and honour and glory at the appearing of Jesus Christ:*

Overview

The Bible records many failures, because it records life as it is. The biographies in Scripture are about real people who suffered real defeats. In this lesson, we learn from the life of Peter that failure doesn't have to be final and that we can actually use it as a stepping stone to success.

Lesson Aim

In our Christian walk, we each fall. When we fall, however, we can either allow the failure to set us back, or we can determine to use the failure to propel us forward in growth. Not everyone will learn or profit from failure. Failure comes naturally; learning from failure requires a personal choice. We must choose victory if we are to fail forward.

Introduction

_____

_____

_____

I.   An _____ of Failure

MATTHEW 26:31–33

31   Then saith Jesus unto them, All ye shall be offended because of me this night: for it is written, I will smite the shepherd, and the sheep of the flock shall be scattered abroad. 32   But after I am risen again, I will go before you into Galilee. 33   Peter answered and said unto him, Though all men shall be offended because of thee, yet will I never be offended.

MATTHEW 26:40

40   And he cometh unto the disciples, and findeth them asleep, and saith unto Peter, What, could ye not watch with me one hour?

MATTHEW 26:58

58   But Peter followed him afar off unto the high priest's palace, and went in, and sat with the servants, to see the end.

JOHN 18:18

18   And the servants and officers stood there, who had made a fire of coals; for it was cold: and they warmed themselves: and Peter stood with them, and warmed himself.

JOHN 18:25

25   And Simon Peter stood and warmed himself. They said therefore unto him, Art not thou also one of his disciples? He denied it, and said, I am not.

Mark 14:70–71

70 And he denied it again. And a little after, they that stood by said again to Peter, Surely thou art one of them: for thou art a Galilaean, and thy speech agreeth thereto.

71 But he began to curse and to swear, saying, I know not this man of whom ye speak.

A. Recognize that _____ is not final.

Romans 3:23

23 For all have sinned, and come short of the glory of God;

Proverbs 24:16

16 For a just man falleth seven times, and riseth up again: but the wicked shall fall into mischief.

B. Realize _____ is the foundation to victory.

Mark 16:7

7 But go your way, tell his disciples and Peter that he goeth before you into Galilee: there shall ye see him, as he said unto you.

Proverbs 28:13

13 He that covereth his sins shall not prosper: but whoso confesseth and forsaketh them shall have mercy.

Luke 22:60–62

60 And Peter said, Man, I know not what thou sayest. And immediately, while he yet spake, the cock crew.

61 And the Lord turned, and looked upon Peter. And Peter remembered the word of the Lord, how he had said unto him, Before the cock crow, thou shalt deny me thrice.

62 *And Peter went out, and wept bitterly.*

1 JOHN 1:9
9 *If we confess our sins, he is faithful and just to forgive us our sins, and to cleanse us from all unrighteousness.*

II. _____ **from Failure**

ACTS 2:14, 41
14 *But Peter, standing up with the eleven, lifted up his voice, and said unto them, Ye men of Judaea, and all ye that dwell at Jerusalem, be this known unto you, and hearken to my words:*
41 *Then they that gladly received his word were baptized: and the same day there were added unto them about three thousand souls.*

   A. _____ *to ask the right question.*

   B. _____ *to grow.*

   C. _____ *your vocabulary.*

   D. _____ *the value of failure.*

III. The _____ **to Success**

PROVERBS 24:16A
16 *For a just man falleth seven times, and riseth up again.*

   A. Develop _____ *hearing.*

NEHEMIAH 6:3

3   And I sent messengers unto them, saying, I am doing a great work, so that I cannot come down: why should the work cease, whilst I leave it, and come down to you?

B. Make _____ a gauge for growth.

C. Maintain a _____ perspective.

PHILIPPIANS 3:13–14

13   Brethren, I count not myself to have apprehended: but this one thing I do, forgetting those things which are behind, and reaching forth unto those things which are before,

14   I press toward the mark for the prize of the high calling of God in Christ Jesus.

HEBREWS 12:1–2

1   Wherefore seeing we also are compassed about with so great a cloud of witnesses, let us lay aside every weight, and the sin which doth so easily beset us, and let us run with patience the race that is set before us,

2   Looking unto Jesus the author and finisher of our faith; who for the joy that was set before him endured the cross, despising the shame, and is set down at the right hand of the throne of God.

Conclusion

_____

_____

_____

Study Questions

1. What Bible character did we see in this lesson who failed and then became a dynamic witness for Christ?

2. What is the foundation to victory? And what step do we need to take to experience it?

3. What verse promises us God's full forgiveness when we confess our sin to Him?

4. What is the question we must learn to ask after we fail?

5. In addition to Peter, what other Bible characters can you think of who sinned or failed but the Lord used again?

6. What failure of the past in your own life have you grown from? How does remembering this encourage you to grow through current struggles?

7. Is there an area of failure in your life with which you are currently struggling? How can you apply the truths of this lesson to gain victory and growth?

8. One of the most important keys to victory is to maintain a finish-line perspective. Do you find yourself easily caught up in the failures of today? What verses can you memorize to keep your mind focused on keeping the whole race in mind?

Memory Verse

PROVERBS 24:16A

16 *For a just man falleth seven times, and riseth up again.*

choose to serve

Key Verses

LUKE 10:38–42

38 Now it came to pass, as they went, that he entered into a certain village: and a certain woman named Martha received him into her house.

39 And she had a sister called Mary, which also sat at Jesus' feet, and heard his word.

40 But Martha was cumbered about much serving, and came to him, and said, Lord, dost thou not care that my sister hath left me to serve alone? bid her therefore that she help me.

41 And Jesus answered and said unto her, Martha, Martha, thou art careful and troubled about many things:

42 But one thing is needful: and Mary hath chosen that good part, which shall not be taken away from her.

ACTS 9:26–27

26 And when Saul was come to Jerusalem, he assayed to join himself to the disciples: but they were all afraid of him, and believed not that he was a disciple.

27 But Barnabas took him, and brought him to the apostles, and declared unto them how he had seen the Lord in the way, and that he had spoken to him, and how he had preached boldly at Damascus in the name of Jesus.

PHILIPPIANS 1:18

18 ...I...rejoice, yea, and will rejoice.

Overview

One of the most important choices we can make as growing Christian women is to give to others what God has given to us. In this lesson, we will look at three characteristics of healthy service—demonstrated by three different people in the Bible. Through their lives, we'll see what it means to choose to be a giver of what we have received.

Lesson Aim

The opportunity to serve God is an incredible privilege. But we have to make the choice to do it. We must surrender to Him and make daily choices to selflessly and joyfully serve others.

Introduction

_____

_____

_____

MATTHEW 10:8

8   ...freely ye have received, freely give.

I. _____ Service

LUKE 10:38–42

38 Now it came to pass, as they went, that he entered into a certain village: and a certain woman named Martha received him into her house.

39 And she had a sister called Mary, which also sat at Jesus' feet, and heard his word.

40 But Martha was cumbered about much serving, and came to him, and said, Lord, dost thou not care that my sister hath left me to serve alone? bid her therefore that she help me.

41 And Jesus answered and said unto her, Martha, Martha, thou art careful and troubled about many things:

42 But one thing is needful: and Mary hath chosen that good part, which shall not be taken away from her.

A. _____ _motives_

EPHESIANS 6:6

6 Not with eyeservice, as menpleasers; but as the servants of Christ, doing the will of God from the heart;

B. _____ _action_

ECCLESIASTES 3:1

1   To every thing there is a season, and a time to
every purpose under the heaven:

II. _____ **Service**

A. _____ *others*

ACTS 11:30

30   Which also they did, and sent it to the elders by
the hands of Barnabas and Saul.

ACTS 12:25

25   And Barnabas and Saul returned from Jerusalem,
when they had fulfilled their ministry, and took with
them John, whose surname was Mark.

ACTS 9:26–27

26   And when Saul was come to Jerusalem, he assayed
to join himself to the disciples: but they were all afraid
of him, and believed not that he was a disciple.
27   But Barnabas took him, and brought him to the
apostles, and declared unto them how he had seen the
Lord in the way, and that he had spoken to him, and
how he had preached boldly at Damascus in the name
of Jesus.

ACTS 13:7

7   Which was with the deputy of the country, Sergius
Paulus, a prudent man; who called for Barnabas and
Saul, and desired to hear the word of God.

ACTS 13:43

43   Now when the congregation was broken up, many
of the Jews and religious proselytes followed Paul and

Barnabas: who, speaking to them, persuaded them to continue in the grace of God.

B. _____ *others*

ACTS 15:36–39

36   And some days after Paul said unto Barnabas, Let us go again and visit our brethren in every city where we have preached the word of the Lord, and see how they do.

37   And Barnabas determined to take with them John, whose surname was Mark.

38   But Paul thought not good to take him with them, who departed from them from Pamphylia, and went not with them to the work.

39   And the contention was so sharp between them, that they departed asunder one from the other: and so Barnabas took Mark, and sailed unto Cyprus;

HEBREWS 10:25

25   Not forsaking the assembling of ourselves together, as the manner of some is; but exhorting one another: and so much the more, as ye see the day approaching.

C. _____ *others*

GENESIS 26:24

24   And the LORD appeared unto him the same night, and said, I am the God of Abraham thy father: fear not, for I am with thee, and will bless thee, and multiply thy seed for my servant Abraham's sake.

ISAIAH 41:10

10   Fear thou not; for I am with thee: be not dismayed; for I am thy God: I will strengthen thee; yea, I will help thee; yea, I will uphold thee with the right hand of my righteousness.

Matthew 14:27

27   But straightway Jesus spake unto them, saying, Be of good cheer; it is I; be not afraid.

2 Corinthians 1:3–4

3   Blessed be God, even the Father of our Lord Jesus Christ, the Father of mercies, and the God of all comfort;

4   Who comforteth us in all our tribulation, that we may be able to comfort them which are in any trouble, by the comfort wherewith we ourselves are comforted of God.

Mark 10:45

45   For even the Son of man came not to be ministered unto, but to minister, and to give his life a ransom for many.

III. _____ **Service**

Accepting difficulty
+ Expecting victory
─────────────────
Biblical optimism

Philippians 1:18

18   ...I...rejoice, yea, and will rejoice.

A. *Look for God's hand in* _____.

Philippians 4:22

22   All the saints salute you, chiefly they that are of Caesar's household.

B. *Live* _____.

PHILIPPIANS 1:20

20 *According to my earnest expectation and my hope, that in nothing I shall be ashamed, but that with all boldness, as always, so now also Christ shall be magnified in my body, whether it be by life, or by death.*

C. Let go of the _____.

PHILIPPIANS 3:13

13 *Brethren, I count not myself to have apprehended: but this one thing I do, forgetting those things which are behind, and reaching forth unto those things which are before,*

PHILIPPIANS 3:14

14 *I press toward the mark for the prize of the high calling of God in Christ Jesus.*

D. Lean on God's _____.

PHILIPPIANS 4:13

13 *I can do all things through Christ which strengtheneth me.*

Conclusion

2 TIMOTHY 2:21

21 *If a man therefore purge himself from these, he shall be a vessel unto honour, sanctified, and meet for the master's use, and prepared unto every good work.*

_____

_____

_____

Study Questions

1. What body of water serves as a warning against always receiving and never giving?

2. Like Mary, we must spend time at Jesus' feet to understand His heart before we serve Him. When do you spend time with the Lord each day? In your time with the Lord, are you sincerely seeking to understand His heart?

3. A true servant is completely surrendered to serve in any capacity. Is there an area of service in which the Holy Spirit has been prompting you to serve, but you are unwilling? When was the last time that you reaffirmed to the Lord your willingness to serve in any capacity?

4. What Bible character did we study in this lesson whose very name means "encourager"?

5. Is there someone who has been an encourager in your life? How specifically has God used them to encourage you?

6. Through this lesson, has the Holy Spirit brought to your mind the name of someone you need to encourage? What could you do this week to serve through the ministry of encouragement?

7. On a scale of one to ten, how would you rate your joyfulness as you serve the Lord and others? What verses from Philippians could you memorize to help you remain joyful as you serve?

8. One of the greatest joys of the Christian life is to be used by God. Describe a time in which you knew God was using you and you rejoiced in being available to Him.

Memory Verse

2 TIMOTHY 2:21
21 If a man therefore purge himself from these, he shall be a vessel unto honour, sanctified, and meet for the master's use, and prepared unto every good work.

choose to speak wisely

Key Verses

PSALM 19:14

14 Let the words of my mouth, and the meditation of my heart, be acceptable in thy sight, O LORD, my strength, and my redeemer.

PROVERBS 18:21

21 Death and life are in the power of the tongue: and they that love it shall eat the fruit thereof.

JAMES 3:5

5 Even so the tongue is a little member, and boasteth great things. Behold, how great a matter a little fire kindleth!

Overview

Our words have a profound impact on our own lives as well as the lives of those around us. In this lesson, we see the potential our words have both for positive and destructive influence, and we learn how to change our speech patterns so they are pleasing to the Lord.

Lesson Aim

We so easily let words slip out without even considering the effect they will have on others. Scripture teaches us, however, that our words are an indicator of our hearts. We must learn to think before we speak and to use our words to praise the Lord and encourage others.

Introduction

_____

_____

_____

PSALM 19:14

14 Let the words of my mouth, and the meditation of my heart, be acceptable in thy sight, O LORD, my strength, and my redeemer.

PROVERBS 18:21

21 Death and life are in the power of the tongue: and they that love it shall eat the fruit thereof.

JAMES 3:5

5 Even so the tongue is a little member, and boasteth great things. Behold, how great a matter a little fire kindleth!

I. A Powerful _____

A. _____ *words*

PROVERBS 15:23

23 A man hath joy by the answer of his mouth: and a word spoken in due season, how good is it!

Positive words give instruction and wisdom.

PROVERBS 1:8

8 My son, hear the instruction of thy father, and forsake not the law of thy mother:

PROVERBS 10:31

31 The mouth of the just bringeth forth wisdom: but the froward tongue shall be cut out.

PROVERBS 15:2

2   *The tongue of the wise useth knowledge aright: but the mouth of fools poureth out foolishness.*

PROVERBS 16:23

23   *The heart of the wise teacheth his mouth, and addeth learning to his lips.*

Positive words give direction.
PROVERBS 19:20

20   *Hear counsel, and receive instruction, that thou mayest be wise in thy latter end.*

PROVERBS 27:9

9   *Ointment and perfume rejoice the heart: so doth the sweetness of a man's friend by hearty counsel.*

Positive words praise the Lord.
PSALM 34:1

1   *I will bless the LORD at all times: his praise shall continually be in my mouth.*

PSALM 51:15

15   *O Lord, open thou my lips; and my mouth shall shew forth thy praise.*

Positive words encourage others.
PROVERBS 25:11

11   *A word fitly spoken is like apples of gold in pictures of silver.*

PROVERBS 15:23

23   *A man hath joy by the answer of his mouth: and a word spoken in due season, how good is it!*

ISAIAH 50:4

4   *The Lord GOD hath given me the tongue of the learned, that I should know how to speak a word in season to him that is weary...*

Positive words are pleasant and appropriate.

PROVERBS 10:32

32   *The lips of the righteous know what is acceptable: but the mouth of the wicked speaketh frowardness.*

PROVERBS 15:26

26   *The thoughts of the wicked are an abomination to the LORD: but the words of the pure are pleasant words.*

PROVERBS 16:24

24   *Pleasant words are as an honeycomb, sweet to the soul, and health to the bones.*

PROVERBS 31:26

26   *She openeth her mouth with wisdom; and in her tongue is the law of kindness.*

Positive words facilitate healing.

PROVERBS 10:11

11   *The mouth of a righteous man is a well of life: but violence covereth the mouth of the wicked.*

PROVERBS 15:4

4   *A wholesome tongue is a tree of life: but perverseness therein is a breach in the spirit.*

PROVERBS 12:18

18   *There is that speaketh like the piercings of a sword: but the tongue of the wise is health.*

Positive words bring security and truth.

PROVERBS 22:20–21

20 Have not I written to thee excellent things in counsels and knowledge,

21 That I might make thee know the certainty of the words of truth; that thou mightest answer the words of truth to them that send unto thee?

B. _____ **words**

PROVERBS 13:3

3 He that keepeth his mouth keepeth his life: but he that openeth wide his lips shall have destruction.

Idle words

MATTHEW 12:36

36 But I say unto you, That every idle word that men shall speak, they shall give account thereof in the day of judgment.

PROVERBS 26:20

20 Where no wood is, there the fire goeth out: so where there is no talebearer, the strife ceaseth.

PROVERBS 14:7

7 Go from the presence of a foolish man, when thou perceivest not in him the lips of knowledge.

Angry words

PROVERBS 15:1

1 A soft answer turneth away wrath: but grievous words stir up anger.

PROVERBS 17:14

14　The beginning of strife is as when one letteth out water: therefore leave off contention, before it be meddled with.

PROVERBS 20:3

3　It is an honour for a man to cease from strife: but every fool will be meddling.

Insincere words

PROVERBS 26:28

28　A lying tongue hateth those that are afflicted by it; and a flattering mouth worketh ruin.

2 PETER 2:3

3　And through covetousness shall they with feigned words make merchandise of you: whose judgment now of a long time lingereth not, and their damnation slumbereth not.

PSALM 55:21

21　The words of his mouth were smoother than butter, but war was in his heart: his words were softer than oil, yet were they drawn swords.

PROVERBS 12:18

18　There is that speaketh like the piercings of a sword: but the tongue of the wise is health.

Gossip

PROVERBS 11:13

13　A talebearer revealeth secrets: but he that is of a faithful spirit concealeth the matter.

PROVERBS 15:28

28 The heart of the righteous studieth to answer: but the mouth of the wicked poureth out evil things.

PROVERBS 16:27–28

27 An ungodly man diggeth up evil: and in his lips there is as a burning fire.

28 A froward man soweth strife: and a whisperer separateth chief friends.

PROVERBS 18:8

8 The words of a talebearer are as wounds, and they go down into the innermost parts of the belly.

Lying words

PROVERBS 6:16–19

16 These six things doth the LORD hate: yea, seven are an abomination unto him:

17 A proud look, a lying tongue, and hands that shed innocent blood,

18 An heart that deviseth wicked imaginations, feet that be swift in running to mischief,

19 A false witness that speaketh lies, and he that soweth discord among brethren.

Murmuring and complaining

NUMBERS 11:1

1 And when the people complained, it displeased the LORD....

PHILIPPIANS 2:14

14 Do all things without murmurings and disputings:

EPHESIANS 4:29

29 Let no corrupt communication proceed out of your mouth, but that which is good to the use of edifying, that it may minister grace unto the hearers.

II. An Honest _____

JAMES 3:5

5 Even so the tongue is a little member, and boasteth great things. Behold, how great a matter a little fire kindleth!

LUKE 6:45

45 A good man out of the good treasure of his heart bringeth forth that which is good; and an evil man out of the evil treasure of his heart bringeth forth that which is evil: for of the abundance of the heart his mouth speaketh.

MATTHEW 12:37

37 For by thy words thou shalt be justified, and by thy words thou shalt be condemned.

JAMES 1:26

26 If any man among you seem to be religious, and bridleth not his tongue, but deceiveth his own heart, this man's religion is vain.

III. A Makeover for Your _____

A. _____ your heart.

PSALM 139:23–24

23 Search me, O God, and know my heart: try me, and know my thoughts:

24 And see if there be any wicked way in me, and lead me in the way everlasting.

PROVERBS 4:23
23 Keep thy heart with all diligence; for out of it are the issues of life.

1 JOHN 1:9
9 If we confess our sins, he is faithful and just to forgive us our sins, and to cleanse us from all unrighteousness.

B. _____ *on the Holy Spirit.*

JAMES 3:8
8 But the tongue can no man tame; it is an unruly evil, full of deadly poison.

JAMES 3:3
3 Behold, we put bits in the horses' mouths, that they may obey us; and we turn about their whole body.

PSALM 141:3
3 Set a watch, O LORD, before my mouth; keep the door of my lips.

EPHESIANS 4:29–30
29 Let no corrupt communication proceed out of your mouth, but that which is good to the use of edifying, that it may minister grace unto the hearers.
30 And grieve not the holy Spirit of God, whereby ye are sealed unto the day of redemption.

C. _____ *your mind.*

ROMANS 12:2

2   And be not conformed to this world: but be ye transformed by the renewing of your mind, that ye may prove what is that good, and acceptable, and perfect, will of God.

PHILIPPIANS 4:8

8   Finally, brethren, whatsoever things are true, whatsoever things are honest, whatsoever things are just, whatsoever things are pure, whatsoever things are lovely, whatsoever things are of good report; if there be any virtue, and if there be any praise, think on these things.

D. Choose your words _____.

PROVERBS 29:20

20   Seest thou a man that is hasty in his words? there is more hope of a fool than of him.

T   Is it **t**rue?

H   Is it **h**elpful?

I   Is it **i**nspiring (encouraging and building)?

N   Is it **n**ecessary? (Do I need to say anything at all?)

K   Is it **k**ind? (Are these words based on a desire to help?)

E. _____ more.

JAMES 1:19

19   Wherefore, my beloved brethren, let every man be swift to hear, slow to speak, slow to wrath.

When you don't thoroughly understand the situation

PROVERBS 18:13

13   *He that answereth a matter before he heareth it, it is folly and shame unto him.*

When there is nothing helpful or constructive to say

PROVERBS 10:19

19   *In the multitude of words there wanteth not sin: but he that refraineth his lips is wise.*

When it is not necessary to speak

PROVERBS 17:28

28   *Even a fool, when he holdeth his peace, is counted wise: and he that shutteth his lips is esteemed a man of understanding.*

Conclusion

COLOSSIANS 4:6

6   *Let your speech be alway with grace, seasoned with salt, that ye may know how ye ought to answer every man.*

_____

_____

_____

Study Questions

1. What book of the Bible has many verses about our words?

2. List at least three ways, given in this lesson, that positive words provide positive influence.

3. Do you know someone who seems to always have positive words? How have you seen that affect her life and those around her?

4. List at least three types of speech, given in this lesson, that bring a destructive influence.

5. Describe a time in which you have seen the destructive power of words. Are these types of words part of your regular speech patterns?

6. Your speech is a reflection of your character, and others identify us by what we say. Would your family, coworkers, or others who spend time with you remember you saying more positive or negative words?

7. What are the five ways given in this lesson to change your speech patterns?

8. Which one or two areas in the answer above do you need to concentrate on this week?

Memory Verse

PSALM 19:14

14 Let the words of my mouth, and the meditation of my heart, be acceptable in thy sight, O LORD, my strength, and my redeemer.

choose to be filled with the Spirit

Key Verses

EPHESIANS 5:18

18   And be not drunk with wine, wherein is excess; but be filled with the Spirit;

GALATIANS 5:16

16   This I say then, Walk in the Spirit, and ye shall not fulfil the lust of the flesh.

Overview

Every choice we have examined so far is important. Each of those choices, and especially as they are made and practiced daily, has the power to transform your walk with God and to shape your future into something magnificent. But this final choice is more than important; it is essential. The choice to walk in the Spirit has the power to shape every other choice that you make.

Lesson Aim

The Spirit-filled life is not a mystical privilege reserved for a few; it is the daily reality that God makes available to each of His children. He commands us to walk in the Spirit, and as we yield ourselves to His control through surrender of our wills and obedience in our choices, He leads us to the best future imaginable! Choosing the Spirit-filled life will transform your walk with God.

Introduction

_____

_____

_____

Ephesians 1:19
19 And what is the exceeding greatness of his power to us-ward who believe, according to the working of his mighty power,

Ephesians 1:13–14
13 In whom ye also trusted, after that ye heard the word of truth, the gospel of your salvation: in whom also after that ye believed, ye were sealed with that holy Spirit of promise,
14 Which is the earnest of our inheritance until the redemption of the purchased possession, unto the praise of his glory.

Ephesians 4:30
30 And grieve not the holy Spirit of God, whereby ye are sealed unto the day of redemption.

Ephesians 5:18
18 And be not drunk with wine, wherein is excess; but be filled with the Spirit;

I. The _____

John 15:5
5 I am the vine, ye are the branches: He that abideth in me, and I in him, the same bringeth forth much fruit: for without me ye can do nothing.

MARK 10:27

27 And Jesus looking upon them saith, With men it is impossible, but not with God: for with God all things are possible.

EPHESIANS 5:18

18 And be not drunk with wine, wherein is excess; but be filled with the Spirit;

GALATIANS 5:16

16 This I say then, Walk in the Spirit, and ye shall not fulfil the lust of the flesh.

II. The _____

A. _____

PSALM 63:1

1 O God, thou art my God; early will I seek thee: my soul thirsteth for thee, my flesh longeth for thee in a dry and thirsty land, where no water is;

B. _____

ROMANS 12:1

1 I beseech you therefore, brethren, by the mercies of God, that ye present your bodies a living sacrifice, holy, acceptable unto God, which is your reasonable service.

2 CORINTHIANS 5:15

15 And that he died for all, that they which live should not henceforth live unto themselves, but unto him which died for them, and rose again.

C. _____

EPHESIANS 4:30

30 And grieve not the holy Spirit of God, whereby ye are sealed unto the day of redemption.

III. The _____

GALATIANS 5:22–23

22 But the fruit of the Spirit is love, joy, peace, longsuffering, gentleness, goodness, faith,
23 Meekness, temperance: against such there is no law.

EPHESIANS 5:19–22, 25, 28

19 Speaking to yourselves in psalms and hymns and spiritual songs, singing and making melody in your heart to the Lord;
20 Giving thanks always for all things unto God and the Father in the name of our Lord Jesus Christ;
21 Submitting yourselves one to another in the fear of God.
22 Wives, submit yourselves unto your own husbands, as unto the Lord.
25 Husbands, love your wives, even as Christ also loved the church, and gave himself for it;
28 So ought men to love their wives as their own bodies. He that loveth his wife loveth himself.

A. *Grateful* _____

LUKE 6:45

45 A good man out of the good treasure of his heart bringeth forth that which is good; and an evil man out of the evil treasure of his heart bringeth forth that which is evil: for of the abundance of the heart his mouth speaketh.

PSALM 34:1

1   I will bless the LORD at all times: his praise shall continually be in my mouth.

B. *Joyful* _____

ACTS 16:25

25   And at midnight Paul and Silas prayed, and sang praises unto God: and the prisoners heard them.

C. *Loving* _____

ROMANS 12:10

10   Be kindly affectioned one to another with brotherly love; in honour preferring one another.

Conclusion

_____

_____

_____

Study Questions

1. Why is the choice to walk in the Spirit the most important of all choices Christian women encounter?

2. How do we know that Spirit-filled living is non-optional if we want to be obedient to God?

3. What does the word *filled* in Ephesians 5:18 mean? What does it mean to be "filled with the Spirit"?

4. What are the three characteristics given in this lesson of Spirit-filled living?

5. Is your speech regularly filled with gratefulness, praise, and encouragement? Would those around you characterize you as a complainer or encourager?

6. Has there been a time when you have observed a Spirit-filled Christian walk through a difficult trial with joy? How did God use their testimony in your life?

7. How healthy are your relationships with your family, friends, pastor, church members, and coworkers? Are these relationships characterized by sacrificial love on your part?

8. Looking back over this lesson series on choices, what are three areas of choice we have studied in which you can see growth in your own life? What three specific choices do you need to continue to focus on growing in?

Memory Verses

EPHESIANS 5:18
18 And be not drunk with wine, wherein is excess; but be filled with the Spirit;

GALATIANS 5:16
16 This I say then, Walk in the Spirit, and ye shall not fulfil the lust of the flesh.

For additional Christian
growth resources visit
www.strivingtogether.com